POETRY
IS LIKE THE
Whisper
OF THE
Wind

JACK GRINER

Order this book online at www.trafford.com
or email orders@trafford.com

Most Trafford titles are also available at major online book retailers.

Print information available on the last page.

ISBN: 978-1-4907-9658-1 (sc)
ISBN: 978-1-4907-9664-2 (e)

Trafford rev. 12/21/2019

www.trafford.com
North America & international
toll-free: 1 888 232 4444 (USA & Canada)
fax: 812 355 4082

CONTENTS

Chin Up... 1

Christmas Spirit 2

Dust Cloud.. 3

Five Tours 4

Girl Meets World 5

Golf 6

Good Life.. 7

High Lite 8

Hunger.. 9

In The Dark.. 10

Jelly.. 11

Just Thinking.. 12

Leaks.. 13

Let Others In 14

Lift Your Nose... 15

Now Just Believe 16

Oktoberfest 17

Old 18

Saved The Day.. 19

See How They Like It 20

Stars Look Down 21

Sure Looking For Mail.. 22

That Little Candy Cane 23

The Dark Will Be Here Soon 24

The Good Earth 25

The Starlight Dark.. 26

Trust 27

Try It All Year 28

Wet Leaf 29

Without A Strain 30

Your Shadow 31

A Ticket 32

A Walk With Christ 33

Another Call To The Lord 34

Bunch Of Cards 35

Cloud Cover That Didn't Cover 36

Nature's Combat 37

Fast Rabbet 38

Gray Moth 39

He's Coming 40

How Strange 41

It's A Remedy 42

Reaching Out 43

He's Coming 44

Learn From Books 45

Life Goes On 46

Not Alike 47

Poor Bird 48

Reaching Out 49

Short Legs 50

So How Soon 51

That Girl And Her Drum 52

That Whistle 53

The Dentist 54

The Moose 55

The Penguin 56

The State Of Mind 57

The Study Of Two Figures 58

Those Little Things 59

Top Of The Town 60

Water 61

What To Do 62

Whatever 63

Work 64

Minister 65

Flying So Pretty 66

Some Thought 67

Don't Gamble 68

A Little Help 69

Yesterday 70

A Battle But Trying To Win 71

How Sad 72

Some Thought 73

Our Cowboy Gathering 74

I Don't Care 75

A Little Shade 76

Joy 77

Oh My 78

The Blue Lake 79

Say It 80

A Good Walk 81

X How Sad 82

Just A Show Of Gratitude 83

Alone 84

The Blower Of Leaves 85

A Bonny Skull 86

Soup For Your Soul 87

Just A Small Brown Bulb 88

A Bunch Of Contained Clouds 89

Walking In The Meadow 90

That Olive Tree 91

A Bump In The Dark 92

Say It 93

Just Look At All The Things That Fly 94

Ship Ahoy 95

Dead Worms 96

The Garden By Moonlight 97

Games Old Guys Play 98

Say It 99

A Little Effort 100

A Hard Rain 101

A Word Or Two 102

Don't Believe All They Tell You 103

Dreams That Float 104

The Garden By Moonlight 105

Well It's A Good Try 106

Crows 107

Say It 108

Little Sounds 109

What You Heard 110

A Walk On The Beach 111

Fresh Bread 112

For The Birds 113

Dreams That Float 114

The Joys Of Youth 115

Graveyard 116

May Be Chubby 117

Politics 118

Oh My 119

So We Hope 120

Talks A Lot 121

100 Year Old Barn 122

Thinking 123

Short Legs 124

That Old Sun 125

Earthquake 6.4.. 126

Now 7.1.. 127

The Wait... 128

7.1 Shake... 129

New Glasses... 130

Xx Out The Window..131

Craze Wind.. 132

May Be A Fire..133

Keep It Our Land 134

Hopscotch..135

Sad They All Went Away 136

Leave Us Alone.. 137

New Glasses 138

Friendly.. 139

Not Just Any Foot... 140

Who Knows...141

A Leak 142

There In The Sun...143

Well A Kid Saves The Dirt.. 144

Stopped 145

Oh Well 146

Road Hazard..147

There In The Sun...148

Good Morning..149

Chin Up

When a bit of sunshine hits you
After passing through the clouds
When a fit of laughter gets you
Your old spine sure feeling proud
Don't forget to give it a fling
At a soul that's feeling blue
Then don't forget you sent it
And be glad it came from you

Christmas Spirit

There was a lot of noise up on the roof
Was sure Santa's reindeer had come
Early to see the way
It was nice they did so what can I say
What I can't figure out was there was
Growling
Now I don't know much about reindeer
But do they growl?
The noise got so bad I went out to
Look up on the roof
Darn there were two cats chasing
Each other around there on the roof
I think they were in love
Perhaps he wanted to give her some
Kittens for Christmas

Dust Cloud

A little dust cloud dancing around
Adder dust but not making a sound
Floated in the wind gathering a bit more
Waiting for a housewife to open her front door
One housewife did and the cloud went in
The house was sparkling in fact spick and span
Well I should say that's how it had been
The dust was happy the housewife sad
Well the story ends with dusting
You can't blame her she was mad
What in the world did you expect the
poor woman to do?

Five Tours

Suppose I should be glad they are sending me home
Seems a little strange they are making me go alone
They didn't agree with my thinking of how to handle
Prisoners there in Iraq
Never did like Muslim way of force marring 12 yr.
Old girls
I couldn't show them any Mersey so they die
Why they want me changing my thinking in
Therapy at home so let them try
Want me separated from any there at home
Guess it's just as well Killing them is in my blood

4

Girl Meets World

It's time for lip stick and maybe silk hose

Maybe awfully fussy what to wear as far as cloths

Now demand coffee could even try a beer

Been asked for a date won't be home at ten now

Make it eleven

Couple of kisses felt like I was in heaven

Now no why mom said " keep knees together"

Growing up might have a problem or two

But I'm grown up now and I know what not to do

Golf

A question came up between family and golf
The wife does a lot of driving but I like a good drive
With her distance is not important but with me half to judge
The distance it's important
Her club to her is great have a group of old biddies, my group likes
My new driver man that club is a wonder
Her club is having a dinner with tea and of course
Gloves
Me I set the ball on a tea and ware one glove
Take it off when I put she talks about some gal
With a big but
With me I don't like too many strokes and I love the game
The wife calls herself a golf widow this life is good

Good Life

We would like our life to be worry free
But let's face it that will never be
We struggle and gripe about everything bad
Now we even at times forget about all the joys
We have had and there are many
The simple saluting and one taken with care
Just needing some guidance with thankfulness
In continual prayer
This will eliminate all your many gripes
that was stuck there

High Lite

There isn't much to know
Well unless you're kind of slow
Like me
Hate those people that no it all
If you are like me I have to stall
May be awhile
Then I may catch on
Now when I do I'm the one that'
Smart
From then on I've learned grab
And learn it all by heart

Hunger

There are things in life we don't like to think about
But we are so well fed why worry about hunger
Food is there and we act like it's a plunger
Now if it disappears so we can't eat, say for three days
Your stomach fells like it's tied in a knot
But after scratching around there was a little and darn glad
To find it now for what little you've got
By now nature takes over so if you eat to much, now that
Stomach can't handle it so it's lost
There are now many starving so don't worry the government
Puts you in line for a bowl of soup that cuts hunger pangs
But not much
Hate to say it but this is what will happen before long
Sure as such

9

In The Dark

In the black velvet darkness of the night
Was the flashing on and off of a dim light
You couldn't tell if it was going or coming
In the movement to slow so couldn't be running
My not moving because I couldn't see if Idid
It was Like a moment of release just watching
That little light
Everything was waiting for the night to
Make room for the dawn
Found out later the light was on the rear
Of a bicycle that was going away
I'm sure you are like me you just can't help
wondering about things

Jelly

You know jelly like jello has a wiggle
But from kids you'd get a giggle
Mom works real hard making jelly in jars'
Because to the kids it's the best darn
stuff in all the land
Jelly goes fast with kids around
Peanut butter and jelly sandwiches are
The favorite mom has found
Besides if they run out of jelly golly
it would be a real jam

Just Thinking

It isn't hard to determine that difficult roads
Lead to beautiful destinations
Almost like after a storm there's a rainbow
No matter how long it takes to show up
So keep a stiff upper lip and smile
Because I'm sure there is someone thinking of you
Plus your smile can be effective to others

Leaks

During a rain you may find disappointment
You have leaks
Mostly where you don't want them
So what else can you do,brake out panes
Now you descant forget to empty them
Or you end up with more wet
Never mind saving that water pour it down
the drain
So here you sit with your panes waiting for
the end of that rain

Let Others In

Knowing your shadow follows Christ is why you can kick up your heals
Plus we know how wonderful being saved with Christ makes you feel
You gave him your life he is your savior we know why you are so great full
Don't be shy tell others in this big world we know they are completely enslaved

Lift Your Nose

When it comes to smell's there are some that
catches your attention
Have you ever walked past a bakery stopped?
to savor the smell
Or have you gotten into a car liking the smell
it's new you can tell
Would you believe in China they hate that smell
Now the manufactures fight to get rid of it
Fragments are welcome and so pleasing like the
cooking of meat ribs in your campsite
Then smell that field close by of clover in bloom
Even the birds are loving that natures smell it
is giving forth

Now Just Believe

Abraham was the father of the Jewish religion
In the end the Gentiles came in play
Believing in Christ and having faith erased
Sin but the whole thing defined on the word faith
God is patient knowing everyone sins
even those that believe Christ was risen from death
Still through only faith yet remember everyone
will be judged
But how nice to know all sin will be a shadow of the past

Oktoberfest

Germany is a century that loves to celebrate
Should you ever visit make sure it's during
The Oktoberfest you'll be in with over one
Million people congregate
They come from all over for good old German beer
Everyone is certainly in a festive mood
Now you just can't pass up all that great food
Plus that shit stomping dancing they do
And in saying that I don't mean to be rude
Those bands play their hearts out and
Everyone wears an infectious smile

Old

Let me be graceful growing old
There seems so much to do
Not cuffs on my shirt or after gold
I wear a suit that isn't new
Now there is healing in trees
The cites keep their bold
Me well I have good health
That's all I need its wealth

Saved The Day

While traveling along a dirt rood
Had to make a pit stop
There was no place but just happened to see
A one room school house closed for the winter
Few people have used or even seen
And with a little privacy I went in and sat on a two holler
It was nice and peacefully sitting and studying female
undies in Montgomery Ward catalog
The half moon that let fresh air in was high above me
Now I don't know about you but I always ware my lid
When I sit on a two- holler just on general principles
Now I wasn't finished with my business so sat there
and finished up my privet duties and ripped a page out of
Monky Wards catalog and get it over with
I was inclined to study ladies corsets and bloomers
And garters for entertainment saving the wipe-off
Page for other pages
That sure beat corn cobs I'll tell you
Smell was bad but sure glad I found it in time
Hope you never have to sit on a two holler in winter
Darn my fanny and well everything got mighty cold

19

See How They Like It

Emails come a lot faster than you want

So gripe and delete them

But once in a while you may find a gem

Just got one showing funny pictures of dogs

Now that I enjoyed

If I thought it would do any good

I'd send some back

Or better yet make my own original emails

Like send "you need an American sling shot?"

Inquire with SLOW HIT THEM CO.

Or 'if you save stamps we should get together"

Gosh it would be a lot of fun but I'd send

To all those that send to me see how they like it !!!

Stars Look Down

Looking at all those millions of stars
Some are bright then will shine all night
They float around but some will seek
But they always work and do things right
We like to name them but then with
tongue in cheek
Have you ever wondered just like me
If those stars might be people that
have died and are just put on hold
waiting for our judgment day
With God's perfect plans we watch
them unfold
So maybe you'll welcome my idea and become
a star there is no other way
Now there is not much more I can say

Sure Looking For Mail

There is a nice pair of cowboy boots
Working the peddles of this tank
They are Straining in Iran to keep
The devils from closing our flank
Now having them on well the Army
Looks the other way
However my being proud of them
what more can I say?
Fighting like crazy here hope they
Remember me back at the ranch
No they are busy but sure like to
hear from them when they get a chance
These old boots kind of gives me a lift
As well as mail

That Little Candy Cane

When a candy cane is hanging around the first
thing you think of is Christmas
That hook on the end lets you see red strips down
its pencil thin body
Peppermint flavor is the delight of children just
Everyone too
Hanging them is nice to dress up the Christmas tree
Only trouble is they disappear like all candy stuff do

The Dark Will Be Here Soon

Listen to the Whip-err-will calling
He knows the day is almost done
So calling to his mate to join him
Now they aren't what you'd call
A colorful pair but they love this
Life they lead
Just wanting to be together
Listen to that Whip-err-will calling

The Good Earth

A plot of land makes for a good investment
It doesn't have to be worth much but sure
Makes you feel you have something
It would be nice if you can grow something on it
Build something or just live there
It may be small but heck you just don't care
Plus the government likes your tax on it
Anyhow it gives you something to bitch about

The Starlight Dark

The starlight came down trying to push into
the darkness of night
The long arm of dark was folding over everything
Nice and fight
Starlight was satisfied allowing a little light to
Penetrate like you see dull light through the
Crack of a door
Thing were waiting for the first slight push of dawn
That soft light of dawn would mix with dark then it
Become a dull gray
That starlight would disappear back up in its heavenly blue
But you know something that starlight didn't mind that
one little bit

Trust

Prayer is a comfort as you ask in faith
We all have problems, darn it, that are
Sometimes hard to face
The Lord will always listen because you
have trust in him
Knowing he is your savior, golly,you just
Can't help but win

Try It All Year

Everything is closed its Christmas
Nice because people can now be
with family
Some have heard church bells
So have to hurray and go to church
Christmas Eve was the time to
Open presents
Mostly toys or even earrings or a tie
Everything was tied to Christ being born
What a joyous time of year plus being
alive and well

Wet Leaf

I picked up a wet leaf that left an impression
On my hand
To my surprise under neath was an earthworm He
said" put me down I live down there in the land"
He seemed to panic at both ends because of the
threat of drying out
It was a concern to both of us so I took him and the leaf
Over and laid it on the grass
There was a wiggle of thanks and then he disappeared
Worms are doing the hula when they wiggle

Without A Strain

The morning sun woke up the sleeping green earth

Helping those seeds that were planted now giving birth

That sun had rested and was glad for another day

But now thanks to natures you see it was planed that way

See the birds circling above the trees

Or the flowers now open just waiting for those

Busy bumble bees

All were contented as they ventured through life

Glad in accepting it without any great fight

Your Shadow

Life is like a shadow
That won't let us forget
Many times we stumble
Then wish for any relief
That we can get
But the burdens are heavy
As we strain from the load
Then thankfully and eventually
want to Surrender in hoping
for that heavenly road

A Ticket

It's not funny when you get stopped by a cop
But it's fun to start finding excuses for speeding
Only trouble is he won't listen all he wants is your
License
Well you have to except the ticket and go home
Only to find another surprise
That darn thing will cost you over $300
Now believe you me that ain't hay
So it's the cops fault

A Walk With Christ

There is a whisper in the wind
and It makes tree top sway
Now with us we walk a tight rope
As we wait judgment day
Waiting to be with Christ
Because of faith we will be with him
So listen to your life as we step with Christ
Not like the wind that makes things sway
Continually praying how our life has
been doing but always in the right way

Another Call To The Lord

When you think everything isn't going

Just the way you want and it should

We cry for help then pray like everything

Now aren't we glad the Lord is patient

It's not unusual because it's always been that way

W expect an awful lot from the Lord but

Always remember he forgave all your sins

How fortunate we are able to fall back on the Lord

Believing in him makes us glad we climbed aboard

Bunch Of Cards

They tell me things get better as you get up in age
Wait tell those dumb people get there then let them gage
You get up in the morning but mighty damn slow
Go in to get relief but wait and wait to go you know
Reach for your teeth they are soaking in a jar
Slowly go down to make coffee dog gone it's so far
Someone phoning this early sure glad for that loud ring
Meet the guys at the park for cards we'll have a fling
Glade to be with those old guys but boy are they ever
getting up in age

Cloud Cover That Didn't Cover

The cloud cover is funny to me a novice
Here was a vast blue sky then looking over to the
majesty of the mighty ring of mountains
snowy white clouds were spaced in a straight line
about a block apart
They seemed to want to rest close to the mountains
But didn't move or touch them
Oh a couple very small march mellow clouds drifted off
But didn't go to far
The sun was warm about 80 making it nice
All of a sudden a noisy crow broke the silence
Guess he wanted to tell us he was around
You know the weather the blue sky and the clouds
Painted a scene reminding us we are happy to be alive
Yes the crow thought so too

Nature's Combat

Listen to the ocean waves rolling
Unhampered to give a thunderess blast
Letting go at the bass of those mighty cliffs
That is always ready to sty full the force
Of incoming waves hitting all those rocks
But there is salt spray flung around as far
as it can reach
Can't help but feel there is a continues
Competition between the two as to who is
Stronger
Now neither one is willing to give even an inch

Fast Rabbet

Dog races are a strange but exciting sport
You can't help feeling sorry for those sleek greyhounds
They run like crazy to grab that rabbit that eludes them
What sleek forms they exhibit stretching out in their
Skinny gray coat going around a long track
It would be funny it you ever saw a fat greyhound
But you know they just aren't built that way

Gray Moth

Those bizzy gray moth flit around a light
Always wondered what the draw was
Now I hope the answer isn't just the bright sight
My reason is it has to be the heat and
they are just trying to get warm
We have no idea where they came from
All you have to do is turn on a light
They won't bother you and are just fun to watch
Wonder why they don't land?
Turn off the light they fly away could be they
go land on your clothes if hungry

He's Coming

There's a great day coming when the Lord comes to call
It won't be fun for some because the Lord doesn't want us all
Only those that believe in him and know he is the only one
But as I said it won't be nice for some
Anyhow look forward to that day when you can be with the Lord
Now as you know you have been forgiven of all your sins
Just look forward to that glorious day when the Lord comes to call

How Strange

A decorator will cleverly install an item
Depicting a bit of outdoors into a glamorous room
The item may seem insignificant but will draw you r
Attention perhaps it is setting over in the corner
What we mention is that of Pussy willows
They are a strange incentive article
With sticks about 36 inch long half the
Diameter of you little finger
Adding to its strangeness are little gray
firry knobs no bigger than your finger nail
Those space themselves independently
About four inch apart on the stick and stick out
As you walk through the room those
Pussywillows will draw you eye and I bet
they will wink at you

It's A Remedy

Everyone is always looking for ways to be healthy and wise
I bumped into an old folks remedy from grandma she says
"it's the best"
Can't keep you in suspension any longer its vinegar and honey
Yah I put it in hot water and it tasted awful
Grandma said "honey you put to much vinegar in it"
Well I snuck in lots of honey and you kind of get used to it
Can't say I feel any better but what the heck makes
Grandma happy

Reaching Out

The Octopus is a formatal sea creatcher
She reaches out with eight arms
to grab fish or man
Not hard to do with its many suction cups
Itching to grab for food or maybe a good fight
While little ones gala vent around carefully
So they can learn to do everything just right
Momma can be ten feet long and liking to be ugly

He's Coming

There's a great day coming when the Lord comes to call
It won't be fun for some because the Lord doesn't want us all
Only those that believe in him and know he is the only one
But as I said it won't be nice for some
Anyhow look forward to that day when you can be with the Lord
Now as you know you have been forgiven of all your sins
Just look forward to that glorious day when the Lord comes to call

Learn From Books

Books are Like doors
So easy to open and close
You know I have a friend
that is a book worm
Can't help wondering if he
caught his foot in a door
Now that door is like a book
there is a window in it
to let in light so he can learn
One thing I ask" make sure
you never slam the door on books"

Life Goes On

Those days may come and those days may go
Guess that's what life is all about
We know some are good and some are bad
But look at all the blessings you have
You have your family your home and enough to eat
So life like that just can't be beet
God is hoping you don't go wrong and tries to
Guide you in the right direction then
Judgment will come you don't want rejection

Not Alike

People are more like dogs than cats
Most cats seem perfectly content
To spend hours in solitude
Not so with dogs they constantly
Seek companionship
The female purrs the male barks
Glad to say most persons don't
wages their tail maybe their hands
Should they have a flee so they scratch

Poor Bird

Walking along I found a dead bird
Almost stepped on it
He probably konked out in his last flight
The feathers of his wings were glowed
Together
Had to pick off the maggots on his breast
Now those I stepped on didn't want them crawling
Around on me
I'm sure I made him happy when I buried him
Sang a hymn now he little bird will go to heaven

Reaching Out

The Octopus is a formatal sea creatcher
She reaches out with eight arms
to grab fish or man
Not hard to do with its many suction cups
Itching to grab for food or maybe a good fight
While little ones gala vent around carefully
So they can learn to do everything just right
Momma can be ten feet long and liking to be ugly

Short Legs

When you see something peeking around the corner at you
Guess he was just as curious as I was
It stayed there quite a while then came out wanting me
to admire him
What was surprising was how fast he could move with those
Short legs
There he was in his green tuxedo just a curious little lizard

So How Soon

The sky is cloudy guess there will be rain
Makes most people class today as gloomy
But darn if I will gosh I got up this morning
Felling good had my cup of coffee and kicking
Up my heels
So let the others do their own thing
Let it rain

That Girl And Her Drum

There should be an island for some music
Why they call some of it that I will never know
Had to listen to a gal thumping like crazy
With little wooden sticks her face a rapturous glow
Wasn't bad enough she was beating on three drums
And loud
Had to admit with her pretty face she looked like
she was on some kind of Island cloud that's music?

That Whistle

Listen to that train whistle whine sure is far away
Looking down the tracks you have to wonder the
Labor that was done in laying those miles of steal
That train will stop at Riverdale that is thirty miles away
Guess blowing the whistle lets them get ready for them
Don't think those going can think about a sleeper
Do they still have them? But the club car has good food
Well better get to milking those cows don't like to wait

The Dentist

Everyone dislikes the dentist

At least until your sure he is through

Now if you've reached a certain age

You may walk out with teeth that are new

He tickles you with a needle

Might even give you a pill

One of the things he's good at

Yes, he's an expert when it comes to a drill

Discomfort comes in all stages

After all your cavities, he fills

The saddest part of the whole thing

You don't wait, and he presents you with his bill.

The Moose

Just standing there on the road
Towering antlerless high as a
Church, homely as a house
Walked over to smell the
Radiator of the car Sure is a
Big creature
Oh look it's a she
Our driver said" perfectly harmless"
She then wondered off taking her time
So we went on our way

The Penguin

Watching penguins walk is more like a shuffle
But funny to watch them waddle
Their head is like a bird with beak and all
However they have full fat bodies and are
Dressed as if going to a formal
However no black bow tie
Babies are happy nestled in mommies
Protected pouch like Kangaroos
In savior weather of winter they bunch
together away from the wind by the thousand
close together for body heat
I think the females must sit for protection
When the ice melts they march single file
To the sea for food
All in all they seem to have a happy life
Wouldn't like to swim in that cold water
With them though

The State Of Mind

When you see rocks piled on top of each other
It shows you I walked there and for a good reason
You see I was trying to convey feelings
Important and wanting you to remember them
As you know it is not always easy to put
thoughts into words
However this symbol is a good way to
get your attention
So have at it life is not always easy

The Study Of Two Figures

One is a female the other is a male
Boy are they different in thinking
We'll take the female first she has
to dress to a "T"
On top of that put on a face like
a picture in a book full paint
On the other hand that male
Doesn't give a damn what he looks like
Grab out the golf clubs and lets go
The male has a very good outlook

Those Little Things

Lots of Things at times seem so very small

But be happy they seem to stick around

We find those little things can build

Into very important things

In fact they may even become an intrical

Part of your life

So don't shun them be sure you help and

Push them along

Because that may be the reason you can

Always ware that smile on your face

Top Of The Town

The elevator took me 85 floors up
I pouched open a steel door and stood
there on the roof
This was the tallest building in town
It was quite a way over to the edge
but the Air was fresh up here
The sight from the edge gave a view
Not surprising
Main street went for miles past tall
Building then houses galore
Oh there is the golf course and
High school as well as the air port
But what is nice are the entire tree
They seem to cove the park
Sure is a lot of wind up here must
be why I'm so full of it
Better go on down but worth the trip

Water

My well is nice and deep
Now lowing a bucket doesn't tell
With news of the drought
It is scary
Bringing up my water is heavy
But having water is mighty nice
Have you priced buying it?
Bet you will be shocked at the price
That's when found I should
take stock
Super glad my well is deep

What To Do

They say money is the root of all evil

With all the warning about there empting of the pot

A person doesn't know which way to turn

We know the little guys will get hit the hardest

Only thing is darn it I'm one of them

Everyone say's buy gold are they crazy

So I buy a little junk silver to barter with

They better not try taking away my

Nickel and dimes

Gosh then I wouldn't have anything

That damn government won't tell you a thing

So they just warn you

Whatever

Those clouds request you look and admire them
I don't agree with them to me they look like a bunch
of dirty pillows
There is dark gray in the center and there are a lot of
them like that
Watching them move around so they can meet with big a
Mass so then they can say "now prepare there will be rain"
You know I would much rather have white mach mellow
Fluffy clouds dancing around
Then everyone is happy in bright sunshine
Oh well shouldn't complain guess we need the rain

Work

We all want to know what tomorrow will bring
Can't help but thinking it's the same thing
The first would probably be money but next
Would be position and respect
Of course if you are at the bottom you
Take what you can what the heck
There are lots of jobs out there
if you really want to work
even if it's just as a lowly clerk
Schooling sure helps getting you
a better position
So study hard before you apply to get respect

Minister

He's darn holly when it comes to God

Darn cranky when you say something

wrong about the bible

Has a wife that is full of fun wonder

if he likes it?

Have two kids five and six but not well behaved

If it were me I'd paddle them good

His wife watches them and smiles

I like the preacher but sometimes he

Gets carried away when he preaches

When I sit next to Betty Joe, darn she smells good

Flying So Pretty

Fast flying yellow butterflies zoom on bye

Where they go I'll never know

They aren't very big but are they fast

You can see two of three at a time

What is surprising there is nothing

Chasing them

Wonder if they are just glad not to

Be a moth anymore?

Some Thought

We all have secret thoughts others don't know about
What I want is a lift away from me problems
Now don't think I'm feeling sorry for myself
You're right I sure as heck am but as I said "secret"
There is something I can't figure out now there are a lot
Of little sneaky problems that crop up but you know
after a while they seem to disappear
So it's one less thing for me to grip about
I have to say "one thing life sure is
funny sometimes"

Don't Gamble

There is a romance in my life
It's my love for Christ
People don't thank him enough
So for him it must be tough
We have so much to be thankful for
As we wait at judgment's door
Because with faith we'll be with him
And believe me that's the only
way we will win
I'm waiting to be folded in his arms
Then I'll have no fear of Satan's harm

A Little Help

Mail can be a real drag along with bills
The drag is eight and ten outfits wanting
Donations for most things you never heard of
Now if I broke down and gave even a little
Believe me I'd never hear the last from them
Asking by mail is as bad as from the phone
But with the phone you can stop it
Would you ever go brake giving to even one half
Of those poor folks in need

Yesterday

In remembering what happened yesterday
Seeing things change you can always look again
Thinking has an awful lot to do with life in general
If you can control bad thoughts you get a gold star
So now you have a clear road ahead
Yesterday you forgave all those that did you wrong
Now look how good you feel as your life goes along

A Battle But Trying To Win

A lonely but stately palm tree was trying its best
To maintain its dignity there in the wind
All the foliage was blowing the only way the wind
would allow
The force had loosened a branch that hung down
With a weak wave
How sad there were no other palm trees it could tell
Its troubles to
as it bowed slightly in the wind

How Sad

A female Duck lay on the busy road way
It was quite aware it had been hit by a car
A male duck stood off to the side hoping
His mate would come along
How sad it won't happen and he lost that
Mate for life
So after a long wait he left and will be
Alone the rest of his life
Guess things like this must be Gods will

Some Thought

We all have secret thoughts others don't know about
What I want is a lift away from me problems
Now don't think I'm feeling sorry for myself
You're right I sure as heck am but as I said "secret"
There is something I can't figure out now there are a lot
Of little sneaky problems that crop up but you know
after a while they seem to disappear
So it's one less thing for me to grip about
I have to say "one thing life sure is
funny sometimes"

Our Cowboy Gathering

Our meeting way out there on the prairie
Securing our horses in a group
Greeting the Cowboys there by the fire
Not worried about the cattle they are
Lowing happily for the night
The conversation of course is about girls
What better subject could you find?
Oh one older joker wanted to barge
about his horse
They cut him off real quick because the talk
That little waitress at Joe's bar has been out
With darn near everyone here but only a kiss
Ended the date
Only a ring is what she wants
Who wouldn't get the heck away mighty fast?
So we stick to our horse and cattle

I Don't Care

You hear of dread and fear of dyeing
But I don't care
Seeing tears when they put you in a box
But I don't care
Ready for that hard climb hope it's up
Then I care
Have tried to live only for Jesus
My whole life he has come first
And I know he cares
So fear of dying "not me"
Now you can see why "I don't care"

A Little Shade

A bushy olive tree cast a big shadow beneath
It is a simple and good way to relieve the heat
Birds come In and out to be tthe heat of that sun
A crow slid in to chase away smaller birds
Was surprised they stood their ground and won
The olive tree was glad to accommodate but
Couldn't help wishing it sure had some
shade of its own

Joy

Joy comes too little anytime
You may go pick a peach that's pink
Or work the pump to get a drink
You hear the flutes of the loquats
Soften as spray
Best of all tongues of the lovers
Kissing not wanting to get away
Waiting by faith but it's not too soon
They were watching the coming
And going of the "what else" that
romantic moon

Oh My

The white snow lay beneath a black smoke stack
Soot filled the air then filtered down making black snow
Your breathing filled your nose making boogers
That had to be picked out and flicked away
Ice that had melted then frozen was black like the snow
Foot prints had broken through the crust
There for guess you could call it black and white snow
The burning of coal keep families worm
But sure do make a mess in making black snow

The Blue Lake

The lake was steady with its evening lapping
A slight pooh on the the muddy edges covered with weeds
Blueness of the lake seemed lighter than that of the sky
going on later to dark
Way off were sail boats with full sails pulling in enough
air to give them speed to get home
Sea gules gliding high up enjoying their playground
Everything is enjoying the lake as the moon will
soon reflect on its welcome beauty

Say It

We look back and wonder why?
Then try to remember when
You then say was it okay before?
Try to smile when they say you are wrong
Now they don't forget for so long
Argue just to say it's bad for awhile
This is what you call wasting words
for another day

A Good Walk

As you are walking in the sunshine hope you are thanking the Lord
We know he disserves it and certainly know it' something
you can afford
He has done so terribly much for us it's the least you can do
I'm sure it makes him happy but hey makes sure doing it
is nothing new

X How Sad

A female Duck lay on the busy road way
It was quite aware she had been hit by a car
A male duck stood off to the side hoping
His mate would come along
How sad it won't happen and he lost that
Mate for life
So after a long wait he left and will be
Alone the rest of his life
Guess things like this must be Gods will

Just A Show Of Gratitude

From blossoms a fragment always comes with a rose

When in full bloom they come, of course from nature who provides

Be happy with those many colors plus that fragments that fills the room

Perhaps you have learned by now, a rose to your sweetheart always

Brings on a smile that you love to see, maybe more

In fact roses always seem to have kind of a finishing touch to everything

Evan laid on a returning veteran's casket that is now home from the war

Alone

A Mother all alone trying to make ends meet
Wishing her two sons had made it home
Not that she deprived their bit for this great country
Loneliness is something that is hard to get used to
Oh well I can sit here and pet the darn cat

The Blower Of Leaves

Leaves from the many trees in the autumn do fall

They enjoy rocking back and forth when they slowly

come down if the wind has a genital breeze

Of course it's up to the wind that can be weak or strong

Then sending them hither and yon

As you know a gentle wind has them cover lawns

Then again when it is strong your rain trough fills

And those leaves stack up in piles What is disputing

Most of them are from your Nabors

But they always seem on edge so suggest you don't

mention it to them

Now get busy with that rake the Gardner quite

A Bonny Skull

A bare hunk of bone that may still have a brain
with a bunch of teeth hanging around
There is a chin ready to challenge with that gaping mouth
Large holes where eyes were that now didn't have eye lashes
The darn thing dared not laugh it may crack a smile
Even at night thoughts float around like balloons
But carefully watching for someone with a pin
So if you are looking for a relict get this friendly skull
These are not mine but are my thoughts

Soup For Your Soul

A lot of people are like wheelbarrows—no good if not pushed

Some are like canoes—darn they should be paddled

Some are like kites—if you don't keep a string on them they fly away

Some are like kittens—they are more content when petted

Some are like footballs—you can't tell which way they will bounce next

Some are like balloons—full of air and ready to blow up

Then some are like neon lights—they keep going on and off

How nice some are like a good watch—open faces, pure gold

Quietly busy and always full of good works

Just A Small Brown Bulb

Someone gave me a bulb to plant

I live in an apartment so planted it in a tub

Didn't ask what would grow but he is a flower nut

After a week of watching it a little shoot came up

With excitement gave it a bit of water

The darn thing got bigger in two weeks with

Nice good sized leafs

Then saw a stock big as a pencil

Didn't think much about it and went

Away for the weekend

Came home to a nice flower

I now have a proud beautiful bright

Yellow tulip

A Bunch Of Contained Clouds

Two clouds seem to be connected
Each are running side by side like
That of a cata -ran
Both were a beautiful bright white
There was a light gray where the
Engines were
Each was happy sliding on all that blue
There wasn't a ripple in the whole thing
Being the shape of a cata-ran it felt
There was a long way to go
Where they go was a question we will
never know
But the ride across the blue showed
Not a ripple but a sight for all to see
As I watched the cata-ran blended
With each other plus other clouds
Went way over to the mountains
Then just sat on the top
Wonder it you can now say
"Now that's a contented cloud"

Walking In The Meadow

I stepped on the flower of Clover

That was In bloom

There were waves of clover all in bloom

The fragrance certainly held your attention

With all this you know nature has won

Yes those bees flapping their wings

Feel the light breeze and you can't

forget the smell

I feel it all so free to spell it out

How nice as I walk here in the meadow

Now Dog gone it what more can I say

That Olive Tree

That bushy olive tree loaded with leaves
Those leaves bunched in and filled any void
Birds flue in and surely bumped their head
Trying to find a sturdy branch
I noticed a couple of Crows parked below
There was plenty of shade there under the tree
Being a hot day everything needed shade
And it's not hard to find because of
that olive tree

A Bump In The Dark

The power went out of coarse now that it's dark
Had to light a candle but it's not mush help
Going up to bed the darn thing blow out
Glad you didn't hear me when I cracked my shin
On the night stand
So here I am in bed feeling safer and it still hurts
Trouble is I couldn't find the flash light in the dark
Wonder how soon they turn power back on?
Oh well better climb the ladder for sleep
Darn my dog gone chin hurts

Say It

We look back and wonder why?
Then try to remember when
You then say was it okay before?
Try to smile when they say you are wrong
Now they forget for too long
You argue just to say it's bad for awhile only
I guess this is what you call wasting words
Oh well the heck with it, it's another day

Just Look At All The Things That Fly

There's that dust that fills your nose
Clouds that roam but where they go
We don't know where
Bees that buzz then make honey cones
Birds all fly around but they are never alone
Now don't forget Man he learned to fly
Not yet to Mars but bet he will try
Everything wants to be up in the air
Just how to get there we don't really care
We pay for a plane ticket guess that's the
best way to get there

Ship Ahoy

Noah only took animals but I wanted to go along
When I asked him he said "it would be wrong"
Then told him "but I'll have to swim"
Well he didn't answer guess it didn't bother him
So here I am just swimming along in life
But wonder if he was as happy as me
Swam all the way to Georgia got me a peach of a wife
Sure glad we live on a sail boat but darn it had to
teach her to swim

Dead Worms

The gray sidewalk was soaking up rain so was nice and wet
There was a few small puddles but noticed several earthworms
Trouble is how dead can you get
Think their earth hole filled so hurried to the sidewalk and droned
Guess a fisherman couldn't use these because they would need
them to wiggle
I'm not that much of a fisherman but fishing in the rain is good
As a kid dug in the manure pile and got good ones
It was fun watching that bobber sink when I had a fish on the line
Trouble is had to throw the darn thing back it was two small
One time I traded a can of worms for 15 marbles

The Garden By Moonlight

That cat followed me out here

Padding around the rose bushes

The flowers had nodded and closed

for the night

But beautiful fireflies flick on and off

The garden is very still

Must be dazzled by the moonlight

and contented with perfume

As the cat and I stand here quite

in the garden

Games Old Guys Play

A ninety one year old keeps always wanting
to play cribbage
I never learned how to play the darn game
The reason because it never interested me
Dealing cards and then moving little wood
Pegs and sticking them in holes
We saved the day, taught him how to play Gin
Now we have a few drinks but not Gin its beer
Then have a good game of Gin Rummy
You know it's not easy to beat the old coot

Say It

We look back and wonder why?
Then try to remember when
You then say was it okay before?
Try to smile when they say you are wrong
Now they don't forget for too long
You argue just to say it's bad for awhile only
I guess this is what you call wasting words
Oh well the heck with it, it's another day

A Little Effort

We should make an effort to visit old people
It takes such a short amount of our time but
Means so much to them
When you show up at their front door
The smile you see as they greet you
will be the reward I'm talking about
You don't plan on staying long but
For some reason you want to keep the
Conversation going
We all know why because you are enjoying
that which you thought you wouldn't like
So kick yourself and do it more often

A Hard Rain

Reaching out my hand nudging the air
Raindrops line up doing a good job wetting
that hand
As I walk past my windows they are drooling in this rain
In looking they appear to be floating away
Wonder if they are pointing as if revealing our lives
Is that a shadow kiteing above seems to hover got
To be mighty wet
Now trudging along in what is now slippery mud
But this I like walking in the rain

A Word Or Two

How beautiful I dance when I come up with words
They twist, twirl, stomp, and sometimes swing as those
words tumble out of my mouth
Then as I look for some unsuspecting victim
Perhaps those words may shower him with delight
As he builds a cleft than adds notes now there's music
Would you believe my quest has been enjoyed and completed?

Don't Believe All They Tell You

Wonder if everyone has the same trouble as me?
With all the advertising on Email how much their pills
Cause you to have superior health
Every new one that comes on I buy then wonder where
All my money went and I don't feel a darn bit different
I hear you say "send it back" I tried so was told we can't take
Medison back the government won't let us
So what I have is a bunch of pills that don't do me a bit of good
Now when I take them I think MY Eyesight kind of blurs
But my bowl movement is full of pills so something is happening

Dreams That Float

Lying in my bed it's real dark as the night came on

I was now climbing a ladder to dreamland

Many little dreams float around as I try to grab for any one

You see I opened my dream book to the front page

Only to find it plank

My sleep went on with good flashes don't know what

they were but was satisfied

I must not be good at remembering

But later dreamland stopped and that smoke- throated

world slowly faded away

By Jack Griner

The Garden By Moonlight

That cat fallowed me out here
Padding around the rose bushes
The flowers had nodded and closed
for the night
But beautiful fireflies flick on and off
The garden is very still
Must be dazzled by the moonlight
and contented with perfume
As the cat and I stand here quite
in the garden

Well It's A Good Try

In writing poetry it comes out always to be as real life
Oh you can start with youngsters or end with old people
But don't forget animals, the sky and of course flowers
And sometimes you find thoughts seem to sneak in often
Why I could go on and on but have to admit it's not
Easy writing a poem a day and choosing a subject
If you think it's easy try it sometime
All and all I enjoy doing it but will admit they
Isn't always the best poetry that you read?

Crows

Crows are demanding at least they put on a good show
There is a big elm tree off my patio four crows have a nest
We have to assume it's a family with noise to boot they
are always together
One has started sitting at the nest and loudly sending the
Others away and to keep their distance
At this point we look forward to watching progress take effect
Interesting but not overly worried about the outcome

Say It

We look back and wonder why?
Then try to remember when
You then say was it okay before?
Try to smile when they say you are wrong
Now they don't forget for too long
You argue just to say it's bad for awhile only
I guess this is what you call wasting words
Oh well the heck with it, it's another day

Little Sounds

How present are the little sounds that we have all
but taken for granted?
Like the whisper of the wind or the lapping of small waves
hitting the beach
Then there might be the rustle of the leaves beneath are
the crickets chirping
The nice sound is that rooster as you wake in the morning
hearing him call to wake up
To say nothing of the birds singing their morning song
all through the day
What a thrill to hear a meadowlark breaking the silence
with his music
A person could go on and on regarding nice sounds you don't
bother to associate with but are probably happy
But there is one sound that wakes you up with a start and
that's loud thunder

What You Heard

When you don't understand something that was important
that someone said
Hold up and think it through find as what you thought was wrong
Now we aren't talking about a dare so look out and beware
Ask for goodness sake then be sure it's the right one this time around
You may look a little queer to them but don't let it bother you
Life is full of people that have a hard of hearing problem

A Walk On The Beach

As I walk here on the beach in the dark
moving sand beneath my feet
Looking up at those wandering stars then
realising how small I am
Listening to the thunder of the ocean waves
Slapping in looking to find a home
The wind sighs for hundreds of miles
Way off those fancy hotel lights now show
a very dim glow
I am disappearing so far in the dark I feel
like a tiny sea shell that had drifted ashore
So trudging along on the beach in the
star light but welcoming this dark of night

Fresh Bread

We love the smell of freshly baked bread
With a golden brown crust and fluffy white center
When its carefully sliced now add butter for a still
warm delightful treat
The labor your mom put in you have to give her a
Gold star
Not only when she bakes but all the time
I think we know where the saying " The Bread of Life"
came from That of moms baking of bread it's soo good

For The Birds

Birds surely have their own langrage
You see them in flocks but they don't
bump into each other at any time
They look like small gray puffs flying
so close to each other
Have you watched them sitting by the
hundreds on telephone wires
Side by side
One will fly away for a short time
But will come back sit where he was
But you know I think I figured it out
Two old ladies talking on the phone
makes the wire vibrate
Guess what it tickles the feet of the birds
They sit there a long time so it must be
A lengthy conversation of the ladies

Dreams That Float

Lying in my bed it's real dark as the night came on

I was now climbing a ladder to dreamland

Many little dreams float around as I try to grab for any one

You see I opened my dream book to the front page

Only to find it plank

My sleep went on with good flashes don't know what

they were but was satisfied

I must not be good at remembering

But later dreamland stopped and that smoke- throated

world slowly faded away

By Jack Griner

The Joys Of Youth

The little one is clomping around in my shoes
To him it's fun plus his way of showing off
Now it's not suppressing the giggles and laughter
filling the room
He will never know the trials and heart-ache
those shoes have gone through
However having him helps heal hard times of past
Oh the wonderful worry free life and joys of youth

Graveyard

Should you bump into the graveyard
Of the school for poets
You will see tears falling on blank pages
Those trying has bent the words that
Were wrong so were scratched out
Commen sense didn't have a place so
That certainly
made the poet fail in school
Wonder if he ever found learning is
so important in wriyimg

May Be Chubby

My clothes are getting so darn tight
Glad their new and don't rip
Guys at the club have to be smart
Sure give me a lot of lip
It's always about how much I eat
So trying and walk with those big feet
Thought a pill would do but just
Made some company richer
You know had to agree with the gang
When they showed me my picture
THAT SKY
We were all born under it but know little about it
Oh we see the sun and the moon plus lots of stares
Might hear on the news about Mars, Jupator, Venice
Now I could go on and on but to be honest I don't
Know much more than you do
We all know if we stay in the sun to long we get burned
With the Moon, man has been there and you take
your girl in the moonlight
That's about it for what I know so guess I'll just look
at the stars, walk in the moonlight, and enjoy that
beautiful blue sky without getting burned

Politics

Now I don't know much about politics
But sometimes wonder about some
that runs
Watch some using mighty ugly tricks
I've seen them honey fudged around
Even saying eggs are full of meat
You know they never look an honest
Person in the face
But to them they bring in race
However money is buying their way
Boy it's sometimes worse than mean
So when I go to vote GOSH sure do hope
Those are clean

Oh My

My gripes seem endless
Will I ever be satisfied?
No one will listen, when
they do they snicker
This year has been circling
But when will it end
With advise that I get
You must learn how to bend
But those low stars
And difficult earth
Seem stacked to
immerse against
Every fact

So We Hope

Don't we fret when problems come around
Now some we grab and some we don't solve
At least that's what I've found
Those we can't solve we just let them lay
Then we hope like crazy they will solve themselves
As we give them another day
But lets face it can't get everything we want

Talks A Lot

A little bird sat on the fence rail here on my patio
He had to be the most talkative bird I know
When he talked his head moved side to side
Like we do
Now what the conversation was about had
To be telling me about his family, the weather,
That was hot, and about the big tree they were
Talking about cutting down because
, it was to messy for the golf coarse
He didn't like that idea at all you see he
had a nest there
When he thought I I wasn't paying attention
he flow away in discuss
Wonder if he was saying "least you could do
Is listen to my side of the problem"

100 Year Old Barn

When I entered the barn, my doing that disrupted the pigeons
The horses were happy; they knew I would fork them some hey
People say it's a pungent smell with hey and manure but I think
It's great
A trough of concrete in the back of the cows has to be cleaned
of their manure
It's shoveled into the manure spreader, makes good fertilizer
This old barn still is as red as ever, but advertised and
painted on the roof is' Try Wing cigars
You can just make it out, after all it was painted 80 years
Before long have to put some missing shingles of that roof
Guess those pigeons like it but I sure don't

Thinking

We always hear people say where in the world does time go
I'm no different and I do believe time for me is like smoke
It disappears in the air
Can't say life hasn't weathered like night grass
But maybe like that of an owl alone in the desert
Hating that passing so swiftly those evening shadows
On the other hand like the owl I just don't give a hoot
Just anguished waiting for the dawn smelling wood smoke
of a fire
It seemed to be pouching my rear end for my endless gratitude
Of being here and alive for another day

Short Legs

When you see something peeking around the corner at you
Guess he was just as curious as I was
It stayed there quite a while then came out wanting me
to admire him
What was surprising was how fast he could move with those
Short legs
There he was in his green tuxedo just a curious little lizard

That Old Sun

He's an unrealy old guy we call him the Sun
As he penetrates through windows and curtains
Without any fuss
All this and more as he comes to call on us
He swipe at all of us alike yet has no reason
For that clime
Just keeps going hours, days, and months
His saying "remember my beams are so wicked
& strong"
He traveling a trail that goes on so very long
Well that old sun must be as happy as we
I certainly think his duty must be about
as easy as it can be

Earthquake 6.4

It started with a gentle roll giving me a ride
As I watched things sway
Anticipation was rampant what can I say
Having heard for so long " THE BIG ONE"
Had to wonder if this was it
Went outside in case the roof gave way
Glad it all ended so went in and stopped
Worrying but had to admit why I was
Frightened I was all alone

Now 7.1

These earthquakes are getting to frequent
Not only that getting stronger
So far just a few things rattle but sway at
the same time
It's hard to describe the feelings a person
has when it happens
One thing it's good you have balance
Guess you should stay still you may
Fall over if you walk
O well have to wait for the next one

The Wait

The Orchard has you anticipating many goodies
We watch little green fruit no bigger than a
thumb nail now causing youngsters to have a long wait
However in the end the wait will certainly
Be worth it
Well it's hard so there may be some with green fruit
Belly aches
Now at the end the finished product makes the
world a great place to live
Belly ack and all

7.1 Shake

Another big shake but they are giving more force
You dassent walk you may fall down that is if
Your balance isn't the best
It's crazy watching things sway then fall down
Next you wonder if the roof will fall on you
Guess it's best to get out outside but so
Many things go through your mind you stand
There dumb
Well its over will have to wait for the next one

New Glasses

Got new glasses and now can't see
Told had to get used to them
PUT OLD ONES ON AND CAN SEE FINE
For what it cost just wonder what those
People think we are
Had them use dark rimes makes me
Look more uppity
Put them in hot sand so they sit on
My face better
Guess everything is getting more expencive

Xx Out The Window

When you ride in someone else's car
The view can be breath taking as you
look out the window
May be at the ocean or just anywhere
Say the desert with rock formations
Or so many trees that may be in bloom
Nice Part is you can look and not pay
Attention to driving plus having a
Back seat driver
Now it's your turn, till the driver
to slow down you could miss something

Craze Wind

That wind has lit up after blowing like crazy for several days
People get unsettled when it acts that way
You put up with dust a few dry leaves to say nothing of
A bunch of tumble weeds
Ladies get upset when they lose their hat
Waddle along chasing it well if they are fat
Have to clean the patio and get rid of all the dust
Now with that wind down guess it doesn't help to fuss

May Be A Fire

With speed going through the rain
I saw the number 5 in gold
There on the red fire truck
A bit of tenseness with unheeded
Gong plus siren howls
Pulsing through the city street
As only a poet pays attention

Keep It Our Land

You can almost see the hand writing on the wall

At least it started as a trickle but slowly becoming a flood

When you stop to think, take a look all those facility mouths

woman getting into our government

Isn't there some way to stop them let alone keep them

From getting in

Muslim will be directing our lives and that is their goal

Have you heard in Baltimore they have taken over everything?

All we can do is watch our vote

Hopscotch

Wonder if this is still being played
by teen agers
My older sister hoped around doing it
She would put a foot down' then hop
Guess good things for ones that got
Well another jump now to the left
Cross the line they count you out
Anger for some then say you won
Hopscotch made you lift a foot
But don't step on a line, they hope
you would

Sad They All Went Away

There was a house up on the hill

For a while it was shut and still

Walls were broken and gray

The winds blew bleak and shrill

But they all went away

Nor is there one today

Speak of them good or ill

What more can I say

There was a loss of wasted skill

In that house up on the hill

But it all went away

Now what more can I say

Leave Us Alone

Have you noticed how many older people
there are moving around slowly there are
What is surprising a lot of them are even
driving a car
There should be a limit when you reach 85
give it up
When you reach 90 they do anyway if you
Go to renew
Now I'll admit we go a little slower but
We still get there
Now I have to end this it's time to take my nap

New Glasses

Got new glasses and now can't see
Told had to get used to them
PUT OLD ONES ON AND CAN SEE FINE
For what it cost just wonder what those
People think we are
Had them use dark rimes makes me
Look more uppity
Put them in hot sand so they sit on
My face better
Guess everything is getting more expensive

Friendly

That black chinned Hummingbird landed on a wire
But only for five seconds
Then scoots off but I know where he lands there
At the bird feeder
Watched as he chased two that were smaller than he
Wonder if he was full of gas
Sugar water is always in the cards and they fight over it
They fly so fast it must furnish them their speed
The darn things go within ten inches of your face
Would you believe they look you in the eye and
Say 'hi" doing it in one place then fly off

Not Just Any Foot

It's not funny if you start off on the wrong foot at a new job

You may be foot loose

When you measure remember 12 inches is a foot

You will enjoy that game of foot bell

Watch it your at the foot of the mountain

Going to a Podiatry Dr all he talks about your foot

A size 12 shoe means he has a foot to stand on

You have to watch old guys they tell things a foot long

With your gal hope you stay on the right foot

Sometimes I feel like a foot stool if there is a hole in it

Isn't for a foot but a stool

Who Knows

When you meet someone be pleasant
In the morning then say "Good Morning"
How you say it may change that persons
Attitude as he starts the day
Could be one person is grumpy but seeing
Your smile he might think oh well things
Aren't so bad
You may get a smile back
Who knows they may want to talk a bit

A Leak

Watch if you see a little leak, it could grow
Sometimes may be hard to find where it is
Water well at first has no great force
Then let it get big it certainly is different
May be hard to plug it up but you better get
To it
Now no force yet but you stopped it
And believe me it's a good thing you did
Otherwise you would be walking around
in water over your shoes and saying bad things

There In The Sun

The wind messed up the blond hair
Of the pretty young girl
Now being a bubbly young thing she
didn't care
At first glance she looked pretty tough
When you looked again, her skin like a peach,
Blue eyes, and a shape that would stop a clock
Oh and messed hair, bet you changed your mind
Could be the sun made it ruff
There she was riding her big horse like an expert
Young guys from all around ached to have her
notice them
Should she choose that one some time he
certainly would be a lucky rascal

Well A Kid Saves The Dirt

It used to be as a kid I hated to take a bath
Now with summer here guess I'm older
I marvel when I take one
They feel so good plus what is nice it
cools you off
Not only that, gets that it rid of that offensive
Sweaty smell
Don't know when the change came about
But certainly glad it did

Stopped

There's a blank space in my letter
And it was important what I wanted to say
Whenever that happens progress
Seems to comes to a halt
Whenever my thinking is interrupted
Meanings seem to change
Then again I'm forced to think
All this is caused because darn it
I ran out of ink

Oh Well

When trying for success and I've tried very hard
The only thing I do is, try to be of some value
Then I feel there is a small good I've accomplished
I talk too much but find wisdom from the mouth
Flows like a babbling brook as I go that rout
So things in life seem to cling as you find them

Road Hazard

As you are driving you feel a bump
Looking back it was a bag of sand
I hit
Other cars hitting it moved the darn
thing back and forth
Someone had to fill it to direct water
Away
Sure made a surprise when you hit it
My hitting it bounced it to the side
I don't think anyone will hit it any more

There In The Sun

The wind messed up the blond hair

Of the pretty young girl

Now being a bubbly young thing she

didn't care

At first glance she looked pretty tough

When you looked again, her skin like a peach,

Blue eyes, and a shape that would stop a clock

Oh and messed hair, I'll bet you changed your mind

Now it could be the sun made her look ruff

There she was riding her big horse like an expert

Young guys from all around ached to have her

notice them

Should she choose that one some time he

certainly would be a lucky rascal

As she sped off at a gallop there on the prairie

Good Morning

If you say "Good Morning" think of yesterday
Now remember the things you didn't do then
How often we have that put off feeling, oh well
We can do it tomorrow
There is a slight problem, the dog gone thing
Never gets done
It's so easy in life saying "Good Morning"
With that we should be ashamed of our self
But what a good feeling when we get the darn
thing is done

Printed in the United States
By Bookmasters